Starting Points edited by

Let's M
Soft Toys

Mabs Tyler

Evans Brothers Limited London

Read this first

Making toys is always fun, but creating and making a toy for someone you know makes it a very special one.

Each section in this book tells you how to make a particular kind of toy with one or two suggestions for variations on it. Try some of these and then use the basic pattern for your own ideas. The materials you will need are listed at the top of each section but you will also need a basic kit of things always available.

Basic kit

A sharp pair of scissors—to cut material.
Another pair of scissors—to cut paper.
Sewing needles—betweens and crewel.
Pins. A tape measure.
Pencils—for tracing. A ruler.
A thimble—if you use one.
Machine Sylko (in different colours to match your materials)—to sew seams.
Coton à broder or Sylko Perle (in many colours)—for embroidery.

To make soft toys you will have to draw templates or patterns on thin card. You can draw your own patterns or trace pictures from books, using carbon paper to transfer them on to card. The diagrams given in this book will, of course, be too small to use as they are, so here is a way to enlarge them.

Draw a grid of squares round the picture you want to copy, the squares must be quite

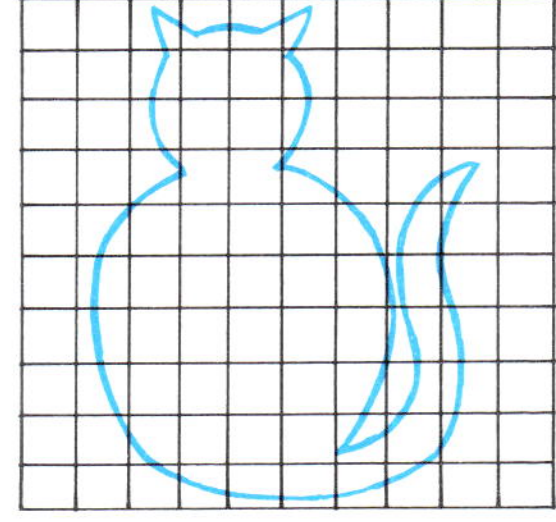

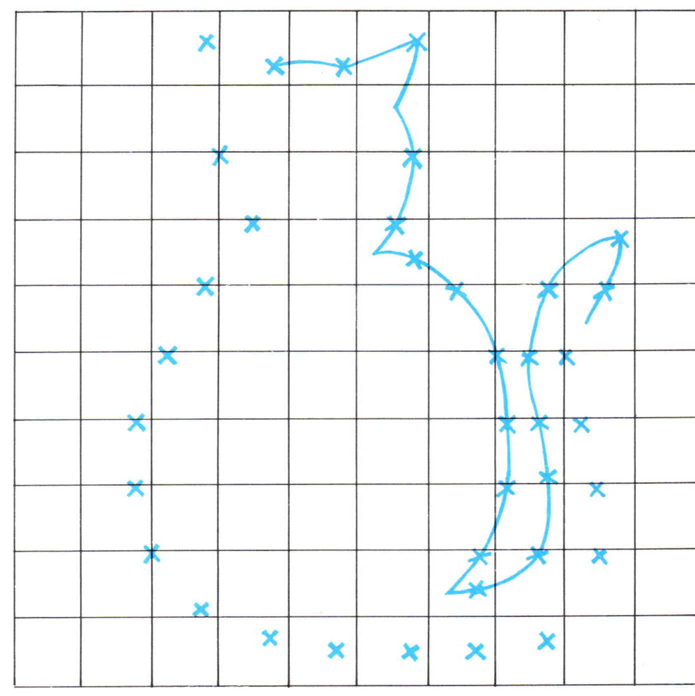

small. Draw a second grid of larger squares to the size you wish to make the toy and on this new grid mark with dots the places where the drawing crosses the squares. Join the dots to make the enlarged pattern.

Most of the toys are made easiest in felt because it does not fray and is soft and easy to sew. You can buy it in many lovely colours in most draper's shops.

On page 32 you will find simple instructions for many useful embroidery stitches.

Balls

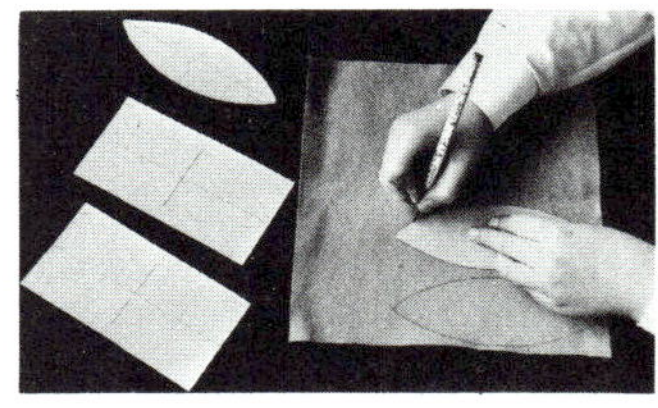
1.

Collect together
Felt.
Kapok,
. . . and the basic kit (page 2).

How to start
1. Draw a line 15 cm long on a piece of card and divide it in half with a line 5 cm long. (Picture 1.)
2. Draw curved lines touching the points of the cross and cut the 'leaf' shape out.
3. Use this template to draw six segments on the felt and cut them out.
4. If you want to decorate your ball then embroider the pieces now.
5. Oversew the edges of the segments together with the right sides outside.
6. Remember to stuff the ball with kapok before sewing the last seam.

2.

Balls can also be made from four or eight segments but the more seams there are, the less strong the ball.

Now experiment
Use several colours to make a rainbow ball.
Make a ball from twelve pentagon shapes using the template opposite. Sew the pieces together to make two bowl shapes. Fit them together and sew up the seams. (Picture 4.)
Sew a length of elastic in the last seam to make a bouncing ball.
Make your ball rattle by putting dried peas or small stones into a little tin, packing it in the middle of the stuffing.

3.

4.

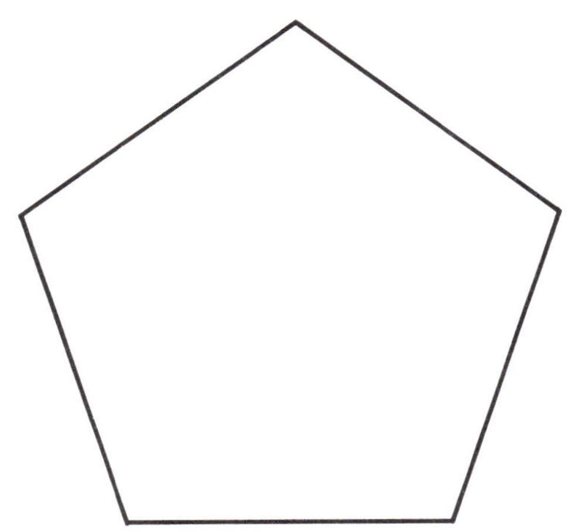

Dice

1.

Collect together
Felt.
Kapok,
. . . and the basic kit (page 2).

How to start
1. Cut the felt into six 8 cm squares.
2. Cut twenty-one spots, about 1 cm across.
3. Sew the spots in place on the squares.
4. Place the squares in position (Picture 3) and sew a square to each side of number six.
5. Sew the sides together to make a box. Make sure the spots are on the outside.
6. Sew square number one to the top. Stuff with kapok before sewing the last seam.

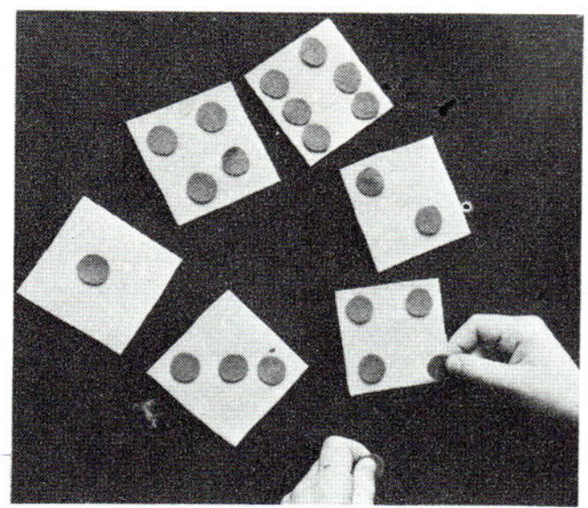
2.

Now experiment
Many games can be played with different kinds of dice.

Instead of spots sew pictures, numbers or letters on the sides.

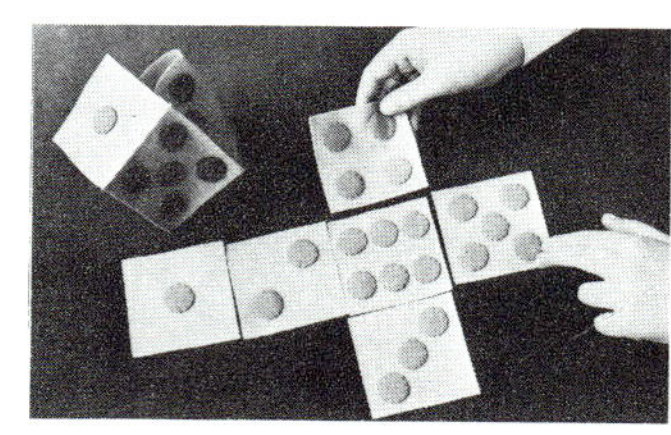
3.

Bricks

Collect together
Felt.
Stiff card.
Sellotape,
. . . and the basic kit (page 2).

1.

How to start
1. Cut the card shape (Picture 1) which is made up of six 10 cm squares.
2. Score along the lines of the squares on the card shape and bend away from the cuts.
3. Form it into a cube, and Sellotape the edges.
4. Cut out six felt squares of 10·3 cm and sew them into a felt box with a lid.
5. Slide the card box into the felt box and sew down the lid.

2.

Now experiment
Try making some other shapes (Picture 3).
The templates drawn opposite (Diagram 4) will help you.
Remember to cut the felt 3 mm wider than the card shape.

3.

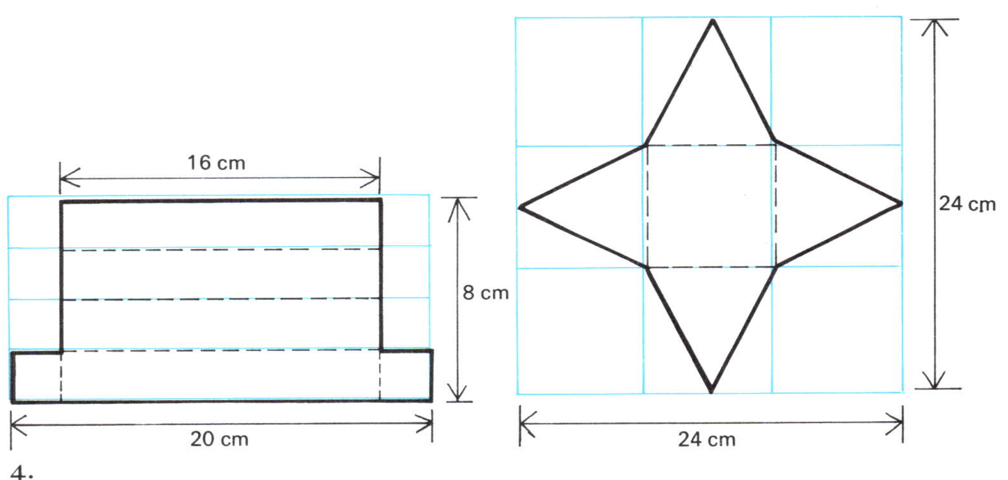

4.

Hand puppets

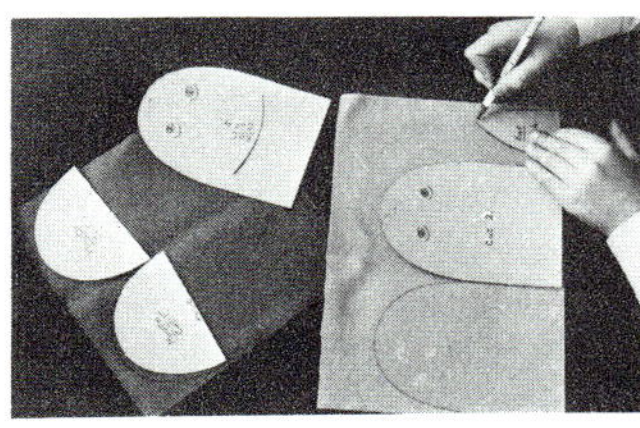
1.

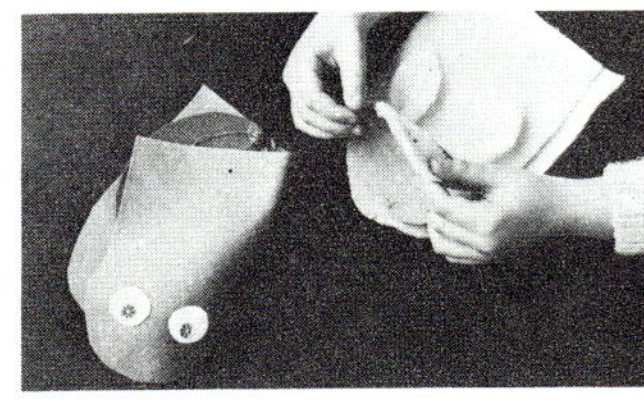
2.

Collect together
White Courtelle or felt.
Pink felt,
. . . and the basic kit (page 2).

How to start

1. Make a template slightly larger than the size of your hand.
2. Cut two pieces from the Courtelle or felt for the head.
3. Make another template for the mouth using the head template as a pattern but this time only cut around the curved part.
4. Fold the pink felt. Place the straight edge of the mouth template on the fold and draw round the curved edge.
5. Cut round the curved edge keeping the felt double and then mark the fold before opening it out.
6. Embroider the face on one of the head pieces at the curved end.
7. Pin half of the mouth to the top face piece and sew round the curve to the half-way mark.
8. Pin the other half of the mouth to the plain head piece and sew round the curve.
9. Join up the side seams.

Now experiment
Try making different kinds of animals.

Use scraps of felt for ears and other features and pieces of wool for hair.

Glove puppets

Collect together
Felt,
. . . and the basic kit (page 2).

How to start
1. Make a template slightly larger than the size of your hand. The template drawn opposite (Diagram 4) will help you.
2. Cut two felt shapes using the template. Remember to cut out ears if you are making an animal like the bear in Picture 1.
3. Sew or embroider the face on one of the shapes.
4. With right sides outside sew the two shapes together. Remember to leave the straight edge open for your hand.

Now experiment
Make a clown with a white felt face. Use scraps of material to make a ruff for its neck, a hat and pompoms.

To make a cat on a stick use the basic pattern, but cut off the arms. Pad the end of the stick or dowel rod to go inside the head.

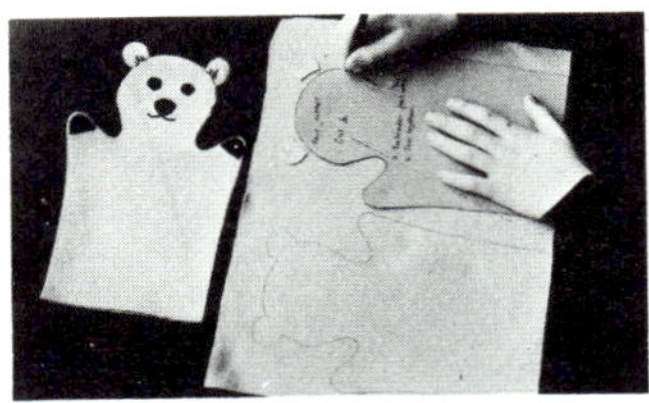
1.

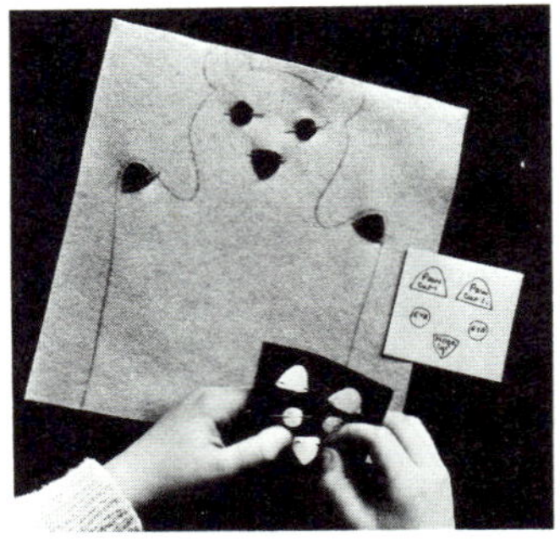
2.

3.

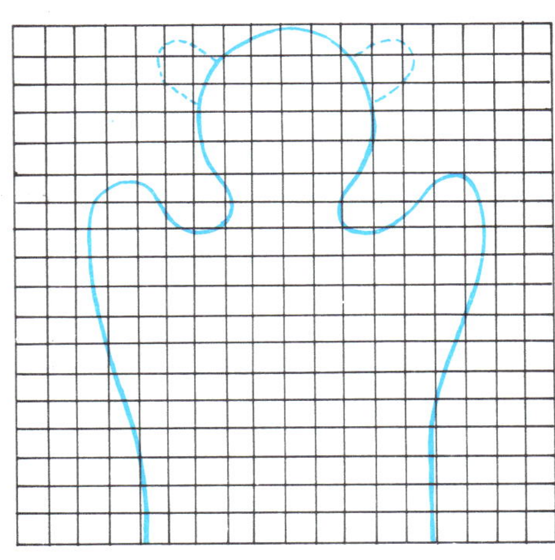

4.

Flat toys

Collect together
Felt.
Rice or lentils,
. . . and the basic kit (page 2).

How to start
1. Draw a tortoise-shaped template (Diagram 4).
2. Cut two shapes in felt using the template.
3. Embroider the shell design on one piece.
4. Sew the two pieces together with the right sides outside. Remember to leave a small gap to spoon in the rice.
5. When the tortoise has been partly filled complete the sewing up.

Now experiment
A fish or a frog or any rounded shape will make good slithery toys. Do not fill them too full as they will not slide easily.

To make flat, cuddly toys, stuff your shapes with kapok. Try making a dog, cat, horse or doll this way. (Picture 3.)

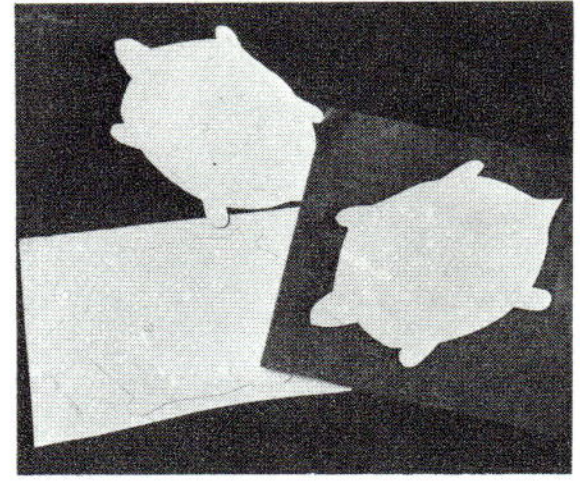

1.

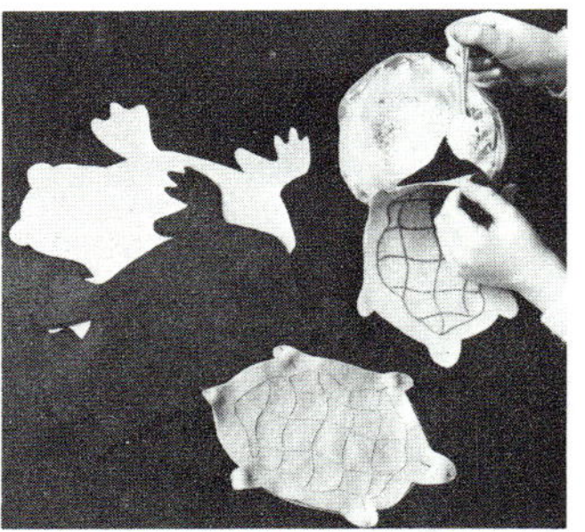

2.

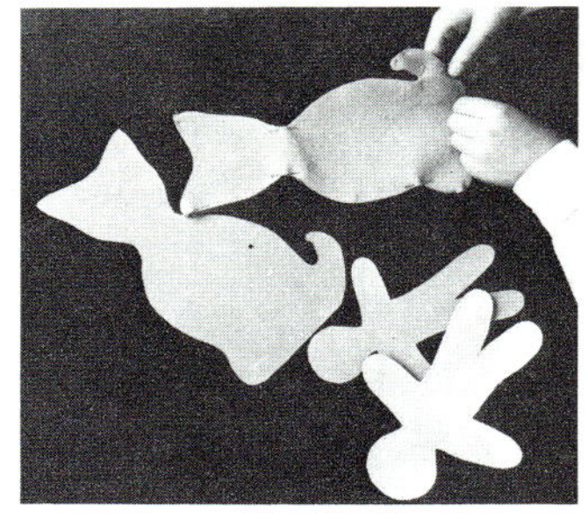

3.

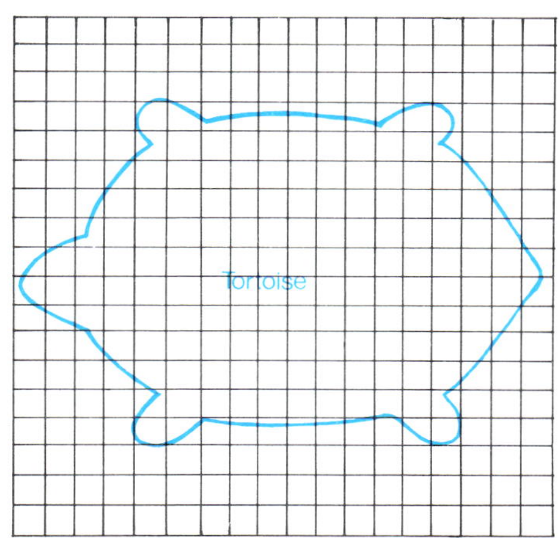

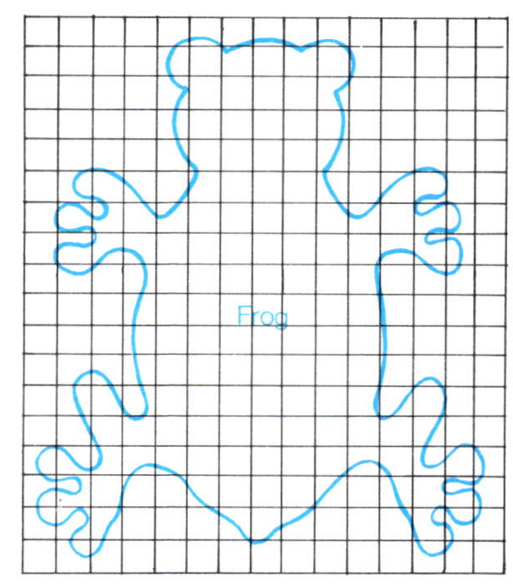

4.

Dog

1.

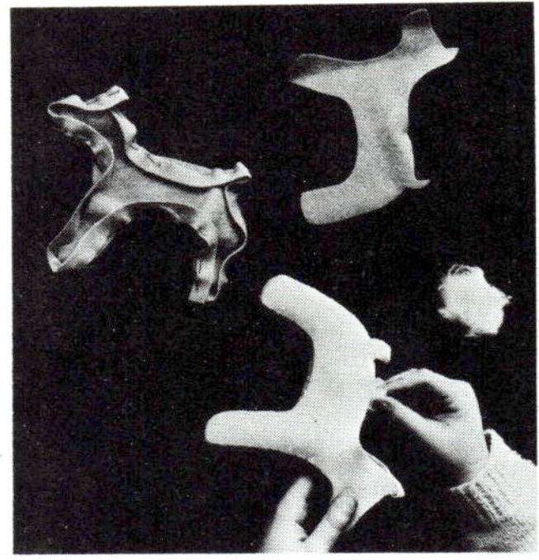
2.

Collect together
Felt.
Kapok,
. . . and the basic kit (page 2).

How to start

1. Draw or trace a dog shape (Diagram 3) on thin card and cut it out.
2. Using the dog template cut out two shapes in felt.
3. Cut a strip of felt 2 cm wide and long enough to go all round the shape. (Picture 1.)
4. Pin the strip all round one of the shapes and sew round it.
5. Pin the second shape to the strip from the chin, all round the legs, to the tail.
6. Sew round the part you have pinned and then stuff the legs with kapok.
7. Start sewing again from the chin, over the head, to the neck and then stuff the head.
8. Continue sewing along the back, stuffing as you go.

Now experiment
You can make several simple animals using this method.

You may like to embroider the pieces before you sew them up.

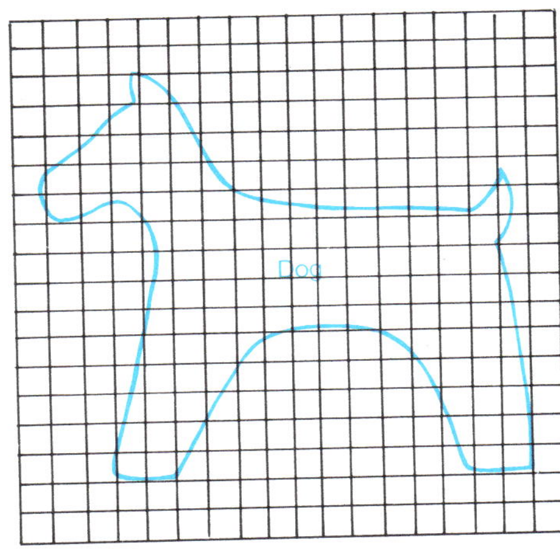

3.

Duck and ducklings

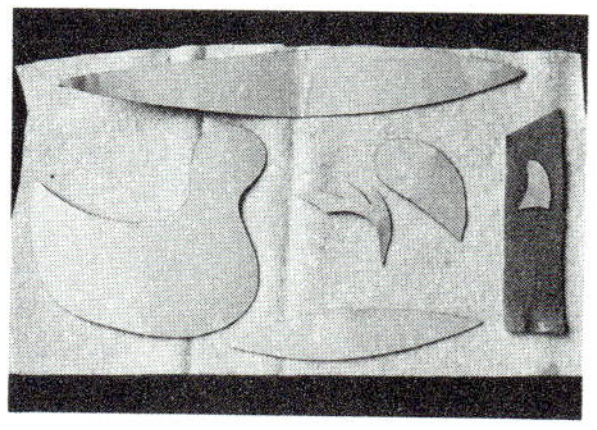
1.

Collect together
Felt.
Kapok,
. . . and the basic kit (page 2).

How to start

1. Draw the duck templates on thin card as shown in Diagram 2.
2. The back gusset is measured from the back of the neck to the tail. The under gusset is measured from the beak, under the body to the tail.
3. Cut the pieces out of yellow felt. You will need two body pieces, four wing pieces, one back gusset and one under gusset.
4. Cut two beak pieces from orange felt.
5. Embroider the two body pieces and two of the wing pieces making sure that you have a right and left side.
6. Sew a beak piece in position on each of the body pieces.
7. Sew the back gusset to the two body pieces, starting from the tail each time.
8. Sew round the head and beak.
9. Starting from the tail, sew one side of the under gusset to the body. Start stuffing the head with kapok.
10. Sew the other side of the under gusset, stuffing the body as you go.
11. Match a plain wing piece with an embroidered wing piece and sew together. Do the same with the other two wing pieces.
12. Attach the wings in position on the body with a few stitches.

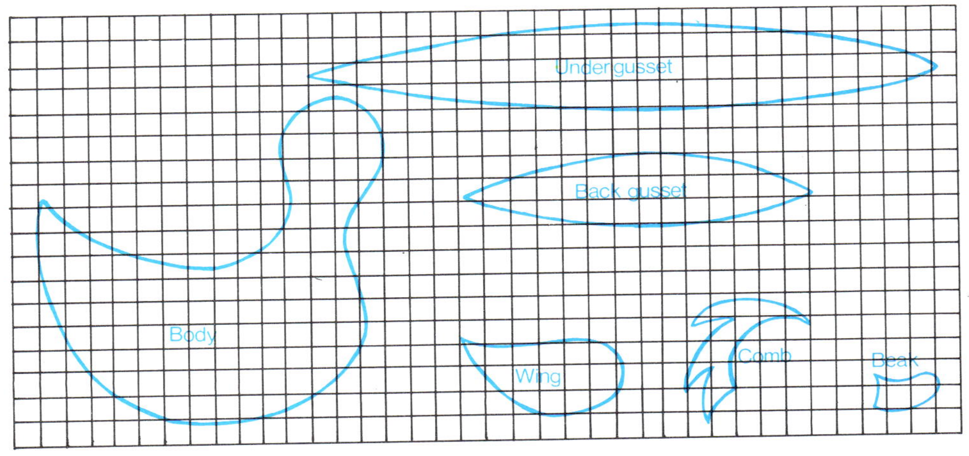

2.

Horse

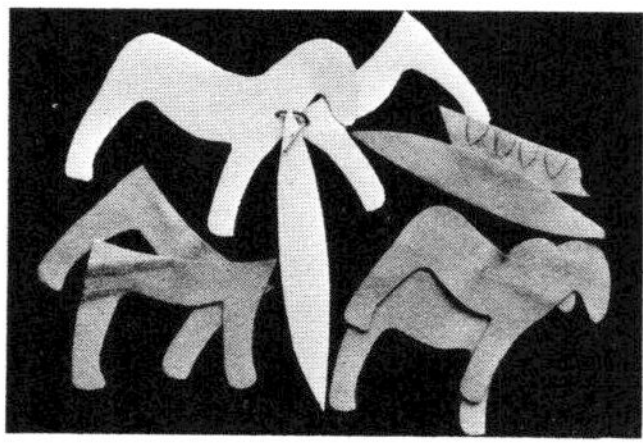
1.

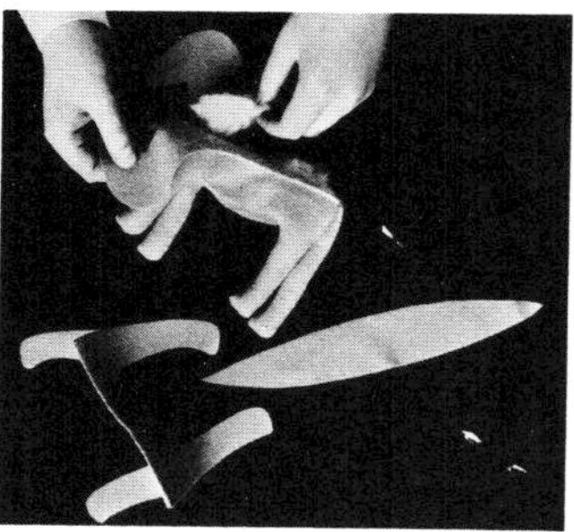
2.

Collect together
Felt.
Kapok.
Sequins or beads,
. . . and the basic kit (page 2).

How to start

1. Draw the horse templates on thin card as shown in Diagram 3.
2. Cut out the pieces from the felt. You will need two bodies, two under gussets, one upper gusset and four ears.
3. The back gusset will stretch from the nose, over the back, to the tail.
4. Using a different colour, cut out a strip of felt for the mane and a triangle for the tail.
5. Embroider the two body pieces, making sure that you have a right and left side.
6. Sew together the curved top edges of the under gusset.
7. Pin the legs of the under gusset to the legs of each of the two sides. Sew them together, starting each time at the chest and sewing round the legs to the tail.
8. Stuff the legs with kapok.
9. Pin and sew each side of the back gusset to the body pieces. Start sewing from the nose, over the head, to the tail.
10. Stuff the head and body firmly, keeping a good balanced shape.
11. Fringe the mane and tail and sew them on to the body together with the ears.

Scraps of felt can be used to make a gay saddle cloth and harness.

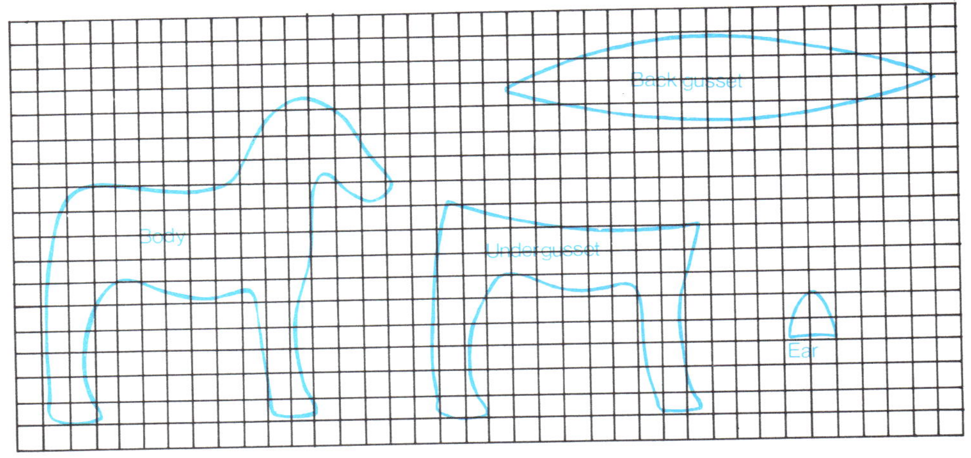

3.

A rag doll

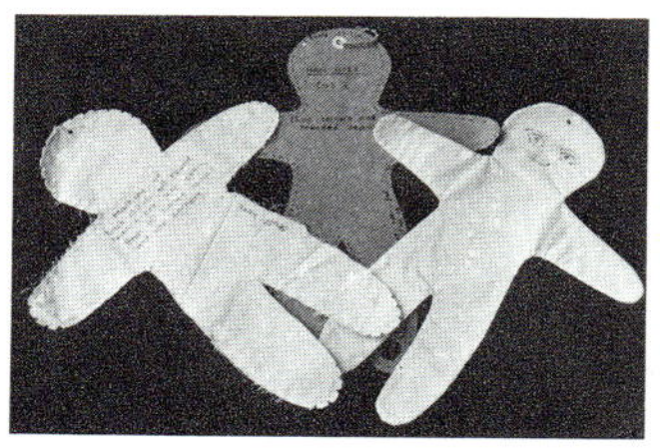
1.

Collect together

Calico, sateen or an old sheet.
Wool.
Kapok,
. . . and the basic kit (page 2).

How to start

1. Draw your doll template on thin card as shown in Diagram 2.
2. Cut out two doll shapes and back stitch all round leaving an opening to one side.
3. Try and stitch about 3 mm from the edge of the shape.
4. Snip small 'V's round the curved edges and snip in close to the stitching under the arms, between the legs and the shoulders.
5. Turn your doll inside out through the opening you have left in the side.
6. Stuff the legs and then sew across the tops so that they will bend.
7. Stuff the rest of the doll and sew up the opening as neatly as you can.
8. You can either draw your doll's face with felt tipped pens or embroider it.
9. Sew on wool for the hair.

Now experiment

Make a family of dolls.

Make clothes for your dolls out of scraps of material. You might like to make some dolls in national costumes.

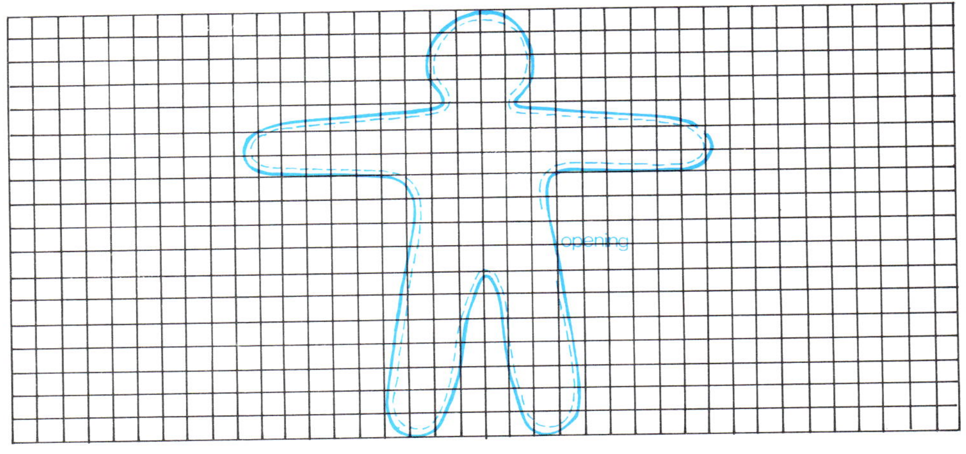

2.

Stockinette or vest doll

Collect together

Stockinette or an old vest measuring 25 cm × 15 cm and two pieces measuring 7 cm × 6 cm.
Wool.
Kapok,
. . . and the basic kit (page 2).

How to start

1 Fold the material in half and draw a shape as shown in Diagram 1.
2. Backstitch all round the shape leaving an opening in the side.
3. Cut up between the legs and turn the doll inside out.
4. Stuff the head firmly with kapok and tie the neck tightly with a thread.
5. Stuff the legs and sew across the tops so that your doll can sit.
6. Stuff the rest of the body and then sew up the opening neatly.
7. Fold two smaller pieces of material in half and draw a shape as in Diagram 2.
8. Sew round the shape leaving the ends open.
9. Turn inside out and stuff each of the arms.
10. Sew the arms on the body at the shoulders.
11. Embroider the face and sew on wool for hair.
12. Dress your doll.

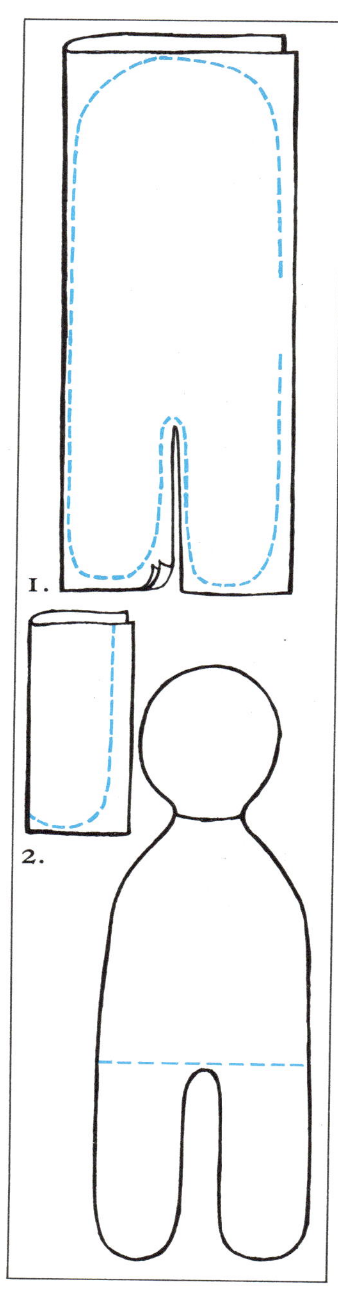

Sock dolls

Collect together
An old sock, white if possible.
Kapok.
Wool,
. . . and the basic kit (page 2).

How to start

1. Start with the sock inside out and cut off the toe at the instep. (Diagram 1.)
2. Fold the sock so that the back of the heel will become the face.
3. Cut a short way up the ribbing for the legs. (Diagram 2.)
4. Backstitch round the legs and then turn the sock inside out.
5. Stuff the legs and sew across the tops.
6. Stuff the body and tie a thread tightly around the neck.
7. Finally stuff the head firmly and sew it up at the back.
8. Cut the toe piece in half (Diagram 3) and backstitch along the long edge.
9. Turn the arms inside out and stuff them before sewing them on at the shoulders.
10. Embroider the face and sew on wool for hair.
11. Dress your doll.

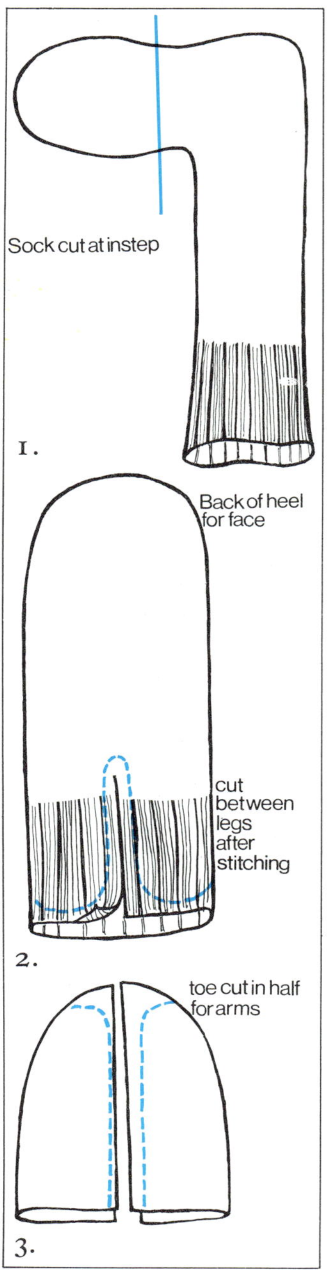

Knitted dolls

Collect together
4-ply or double knitting wool.
Kapok.
Three number 10 knitting needles,
. . . and the basic kit (page 2).

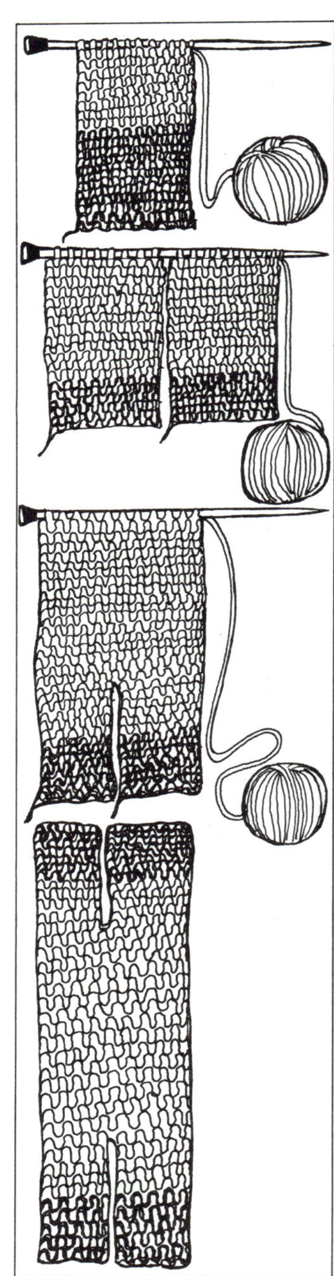

How to start
The instructions given are for a large doll. The instructions for smaller sizes are given in brackets.

Legs
1. Cast on 10 (8, 6) stitches and knit in garter stitch, which is plain every row, for 11(7, 5) cm.
2. Knit another leg to match.

Body
3. With both legs on one needle, knit right across to join them together.
4. Carry on knitting until the strip measures 35 (25, 19) cm long. This will be the front, head and back.
5. Divide the stitches in half for the back of the legs. Using half of the stitches, knit 11 (7, 5) cm and then cast off.
6. Rejoin the wool to the remaining half of the stitches and knit the second leg to match.

Arms
7. Cast on 16 (14, 12) stitches and knit in garter stitch for 7 (5, 4) cm. Cast off.
8. Knit another arm to match.

To make up

1. Fold the strip in half and oversew round the edge (Diagram 1). Round off the corners of the ends of the legs for feet. If you are making an animal with ears, leave the corners by the fold square. If you are making a doll round off the corners.
2. Turn it inside out. Sew across the corners of the head for ears if you are making an animal.
3. Stuff the head firmly and then tie it tightly round the neck with a piece of wool.
4. Stuff the rest of the body and legs and sew up the opening.
5. Sew up the side seams of the arms, rounding off the corners for hands as Diagram 2.
6. Turn the arms inside out and stuff with kapok.
7. Sew the arms on to the body at the shoulders.
8. Embroider the face.

Now experiment

Try knitting a doll in different coloured wools. Diagram 3 will help you with the measurements for the different colours to make a boy doll.

Try knitting skirts and jackets, hats and helmets to dress your dolls.

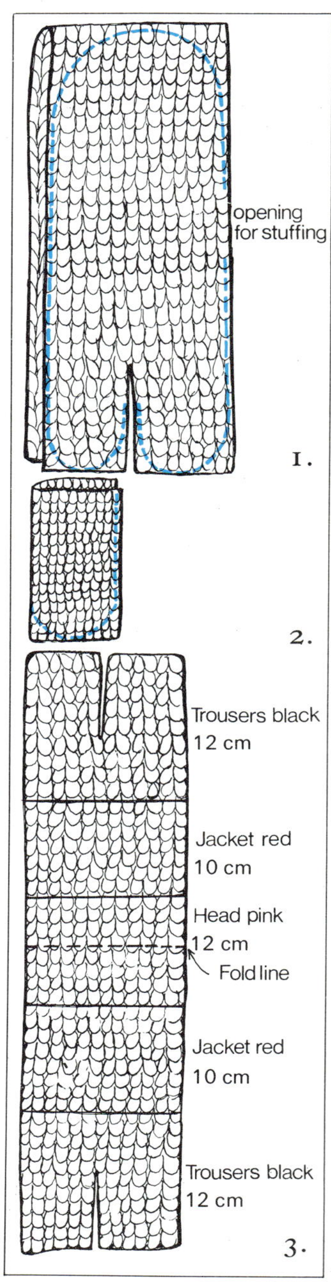

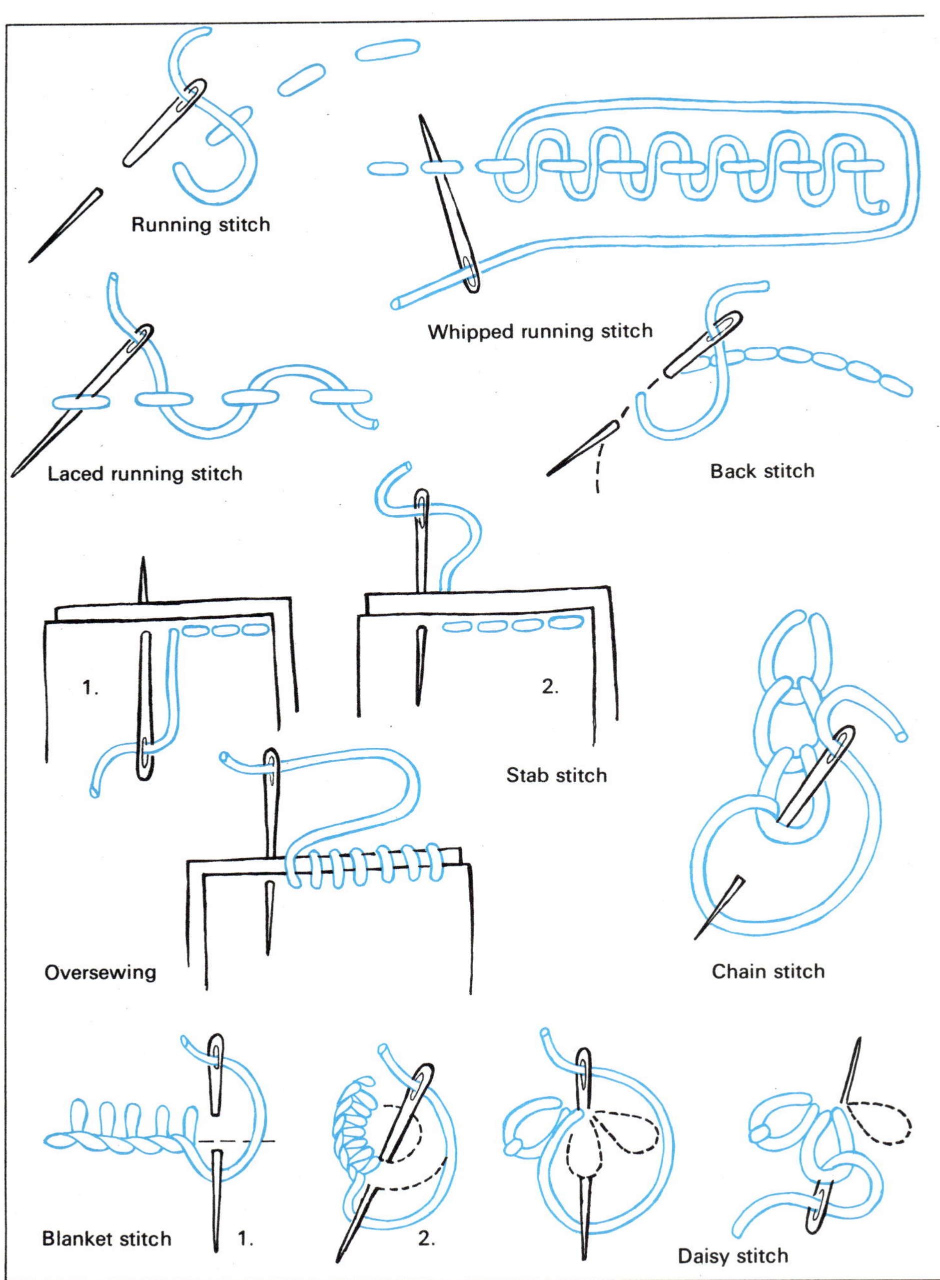
Running stitch
Whipped running stitch
Laced running stitch
Back stitch
1.
2.
Stab stitch
Oversewing
Chain stitch
Blanket stitch
1.
2.
Daisy stitch